Teen Talk

Modern Monologues for Teenage Girls

TEEN TALK
MODERN MONOLOGUES
for
TEENAGE GIRLS

Susan Pomerance

Dramaline Publications
36-851 Palm View Road
Rancho Mirage, CA 92270

Library of Congress Control Number: 2202115114

Cover art by Ann Chang

This book is printed on paper that meets the requirements of the American Standard of Permanence of paper for printed library material.

CONTENTS

BILLIE

Her father, a drunken, overbearing sadist, had brutalized her and her mother for years to the point it could no longer be endured, causing Billie to, finally, retaliate in an act of manslaughter. Here, nearly hysterical, she pours out her feelings to the police:

I was alone in the kitchen when he came back. He'd been out drinking like always. It was like this almost every night. He'd come home from work late and eat and then go out and drink with his friends. Till all hours. When he came back he was an animal. You could see the hate in him. Feel it. Smell it. He wasn't human at this point. The look in his eyes. It was . . . God! (*She breaks. Recovers somewhat. Wiping her eyes.*) I'll be all right . . . it was this way for years. We could never figure him out, Mother and I. We didn't know what was behind it. All we knew was that he was a brutal son of a bitch. He beat Mom so bad once she couldn't walk for days. She always wore long sleeves to cover up the black and blue marks. Once he hit me across my back so hard with a coat-hanger wire I had a welt for two months.

We lived in fear every day. You never knew when he was going to explode—go crazy. We were scared to death of him. He told us he'd kill us if we went to the police. Like I said . . . I was in the kitchen when he got back last night. Making some toast. When he came in the back door I knew it was trouble because the first thing he did was slam the door so hard the glass shattered. He yelled at me. "What the hell you doing up so late, you f-ing little bitch?" When I didn't answer him, he grabbed me by the arm and threw me into the refrigerator. He was . . . he was a wild man. Why? I mean . . . what had I done? Then he grabbed me by the throat and dragged me around the kitchen like I was a rag doll, shaking me, screaming. He backed me into the kitchen counter, choking me. I couldn't breathe. When he finally let me go he sat at the kitchen table. "You're just like your mother. You're both whores. Get me a beer," he said.

I saw him sitting there. His back to me. And I hated him. I can't tell you how much . . . I hated him. *Hated* him. So I took a knife from the counter and stabbed him. When he turned around screaming, I stabbed him again. And again. And again. He fell forward on the floor and I knew I'd killed him. And I wasn't sorry.

This is the sad part . . . I'm not sorry.

LAUREN

Lauren's mother is obsessed with her hair and seems to be eternally unhappy about its length, style, shape and color. Here Lauren attempts to reason with her regarding her hair fixation:

You'd better cool it. You know what happened the last time you went and blew a fortune on a new beautician. She cut too much off and you were uptight about it for months—ran around wearing a ball cap. So you'd better lay back. Take it easy. Okay? (*Pause.*) So it's out of date, so what? Besides, who says it is? (*Pause.*) Doris Weaver? Don't listen to Doris Weaver, for crap's sake. What does she know about hair or style or anything else, for that matter? Doris Weaver's a mess. She has more hair on her legs than you have on your head. Doris Weaver's gross. (*Pause.*) The color's fine. (*Pause.*) Ash Brown? You kidding? You'll look like a big mouse. Keep your hair light. Dark hair'll screw up your skin tones. Stay with the Platinum Blonde, okay? I like you as a blonde. Everyone likes you as a blonde. (*Pause.*) No, no. The cut's fine. (*Pause.*) Mom, you're not a teenager, okay? You get a spike cut, I'm not being seen with you. And Dad . . . forget it. Dad's not into what's happening today. He still plays LPs, for God's sake.

Do you ever stop to realize how hung up you are on your hair? Mom . . . hair with you just isn't hair—it's a way of life. How many hours a day do you spend messing with the stuff, anyhow? Two, three? (*Pause.*) I know hair's important to you, but this isn't normal. Besides, your hair's fine. Most women would kill for a head of hair like yours. (*Pause.*) Now what're you doing? (*Pause.*) Will you stop it? Put that iron down. Don't straighten it. That looks awful. You look like George Washington. Look, you can't go wanting to change style and color and cut with every damned *Cosmo* you read.

Okay, look, here's the idea. I got the answer. It's this radical new concept called . . . acting your age.

REESE

New styles are cool, but expensive, so Reese has dug to the back of her closet for "vintage" rags. Satisfied that she is styling, she promotes her old-new look to friend Cindy.

I went and looked at the new styles and it's, like, I can't afford this every year. I mean, the prices are off the charts, you know. So, I'm thinking, Why am I'm killing my budget every year when I got this whole closet full of neat old junk, right?

I didn't realize—had no idea—I don't think any of us do, what we've got buried in the back of our closets. New styles come on the market, we run out and buy them and push the old stuff back and it builds up and doesn't get worn because we're a bunch of total new clothes junkies because this is what's in the magazines and on TV. C'mon, what are we here, anyway, a bunch of robots for the advertising business, or something? I don't *think* so. Least, not me.

So I go in my closet and this is what I found. It was like digging through a treasure chest. (*Displaying herself.*) Whaddaya think? Not bad for leftovers, huh? With no sweat, I come up with a total grunge look for no money. The jeans are frayed at the bottoms, but so what? This is happening. This old Gap sweatshirt is perfect over this faded-denim thing I bought more than three years ago at that shop that went out of business because the owner was spying on girls in the dressing rooms. Remember? What a perv.

These sandals I found in the bottom of my gym bag. I used to wear them at the pool, but so what? Sandals are sandals. The scarf was a gift to my mom who handed it down to me and I threw it in the top of my wardrobe last summer. I looks really old, but that's new. You know . . . vintage. Today junk is vintage.

I'll bet you most of our buddies have all kinds of neat clothes they've forgotten about. Okay, so whaddaya think, Cindy? (*Spinning around.*) Is this total grunge, or what?

SHANNON

An act of sexual indiscretion has resulted in Shannon testing HIV-positive. Here she pours out her feelings to her best friend, Tawanda:

I don't know why I did it. It was crazy. After we had sex, I was like, "I can't believe I did that." I didn't give a thought to getting pregnant or getting AIDS. Then I come home the other afternoon and there he was—Keshan, all over TV. I couldn't believe it. He'd known he was HIV-positive and had passed it on to a bunch of girls. A chill went through me. A couple of days later a health nurse came to my homeroom and took me to a clinic. A week later they told me I'd tested positive. It was awful. I kept seeing myself dead and started thinking about my own funeral. When I told Mom, we both broke down and cried. But she was understanding and is being super supportive.

I have HIV. I'm infected. All because of five minutes of stupidity. My whole life has been changed. One minute I'm fine, the next I'm thinking about dying. They want me to take medicine because they say I'll live longer if I do, but they carry all kinds of side effects. But I guess I'm going to have to take it eventually. If I wanna have a chance at living, that is.

You're the only friend I've told. I don't think the rest will understand. I mean . . . they'll either stay away because they won't understand it's an illness, because there's still this stigma, or they'll give me all this phony pity. I don't know what to do. I'm scared. I don't wanna die. And I'm mad as hell too. Mostly mad at myself for goofing up. And real mad at Keshan. Hell, he didn't care if any of the girls he had sex with lived or died. He didn't care about anyone but himself.

I never ever thought this would happen to me. I was so damned stupid. I really didn't understand how easy you could get AIDS. I didn't pay attention, take time to get educated.

I don't know if I'll finish school or not. Right now I can't think too much about the future. Even though having HIV doesn't mean my life is over, it sure makes me think about how much time I have left.

COLLEEN

Colleen understands the perils of nepotism.

Dad, we have to talk. (*Pause.*) Yes, right now. We gotta talk. Look . . . I know you want to do the right thing and everything, and I appreciate it, but . . . well . . . I don't think me working for you is a very good idea. (*Pause.*) Why? Because I'm just not another employee, ya know. Any way you look at it, I'm still your daughter. (*Pause.*) Yeah, I know, but it's still different. You wouldn't treat an outsider like you treat me. (*Pause.*) But you do. I guess you just can't see it. This is what I'm talking about. You're never gonna relate to me like you would a stranger. (*Pause.*) I know you don't do me any favors, I know this. In fact, this is one of the problems—you're harder on me than the other girls. (*Pause.*) Yes, you are. I don't even have time for my homework. And I understand this. You're piling it on because you wanna prove to the others you're not playing favorites. (*Pause.*) It's the truth. Face it.

And another thing. How you think this makes the other women feel? They're nice enough, but I can tell they resent me. (*Pause.*) I'm *not* paranoid. I can feel it. I'd feel the same way if I'd been on the job for years and alluva sudden the

9

boss's daughter shows up. This is natural. And how about women like Madalyn? We're both doing the same job, right? What you think this says to her? God, Dad, she's been here over eight years. Who you think's gonna get the raises and promotions when I start full time? (*Pause*.) That's not true. You know and I know it'll be me. Look, I'm not trying to be a hero here, but this isn't fair. To me *or* Madalyn. Unfair to me because I don't deserve it, and unfair to her because she does. (*Pause*.) Okay, but this is how I feel. So this is the reason I'm going to quit. (*Pause*.) Sorry, but I've made up my mind. I'm outta here in two weeks. It'll be better for both of us.

And this way I won't flunk algebra.

GEORGIA

A victim of house hunting, Georgia has more perspective regarding the process than her parents.

My mom and dad have been house hunting. They go through the real estate section of the paper on the weekends and drive around looking at places. They always drag me along because the say it's important I like the neighborhood, which is bull because when we moved here they could've cared less about me leaving my school and my buds. Thank God we moved in next to you, Shana. I think they want me along because, as the say, misery loves company.

This weekend we looked at at least ten houses with this real estate guy who was a major weasel. I was wearing a mid-riff and my low-riders and he kept scoping out my butt and belly button. Gur-ross! I've figured out the difference between selling used cars and real estate—the price of homes is higher. All the rest is the same. Real estate people are a bunch of high-pressure geeks. Every house the guy showed us there was always all this interest, people were flying in to see it. Like, sure. The only thing flying in was termites.

And get his rap: He'd lead us into a kitchen and he'd say, (*Gesturing as she relates.*) "Here's your kitchen." He'd take us into a master bedroom and say, "Here's your master bedroom." He'd show us a patio and say, "Here's your patio." As if we couldn't see a kitchen was a kitchen, a master bedroom was a master bedroom, a patio was a patio. Nooo kidding! And, oh yeah, everything was massive. (*Demonstrating.*) "Here's your massive den. Here's your massive two-car garage. Here's your massive formal dining room." The only thing massive was this fools waist line.

In one house all these weird people were hunched in a little room watching TV and smoking. They looked like monkeys. In another place there was this little old woman in a grungy kimono carrying a dog with no hair. I left on this one.

The rest of the day I waited in the car.

REGGIE

*Reggie is not ready for a "relationship." Not only is she not
ready, she also hates the term.*

(With a grocery bag in her arms.) Look here, Roger, I'm in a
good place right now. Okay? I don't need a long-term thing, a
super-commitment. I'm not ready for it. So, *puleeze*—stop
bugging me. I'm totally not ready to make it a steady thing.
(Pause.) Oh, no. Puleeze. I hate the term "relationship." It's
overused and meaningless. What the hell's it mean, anyhow?
Why don't people just come out and say what they mean? How
'bout, "Let's go steady"? How 'bout, "I really like you more
than anything and want to be with you all the time"? How
'bout, "I'm jealous of you and want to tie you up and put you
in the trunk of my car so no one else can get to you so I can
own you"? I'm totally fed up with the relationship thing.

The only relationships I know about are, like, my uncle Dan
is a relative, my sister, my mom and dad—they're relatives.
When we go to the family reunions, I *really* have relationships.
Relationship is total TV-psychologist BS like, "Look at yourself," or, "Get to know the real you." When my mom and dad
dated, they just *went* together. Today, nobody goes together,

they have a "relationships." Well . . . I don't want a relationship. A part-time boyfriend, maybe, but no relationship. If you're dying to have a relationship, Roger, join the Boy Scouts.

You know what I think? I think people have "relationships" so they can walk away any time they want. "See ya later. I'm outta here. Bye-bye, babe." When they wanna split, they just do, because they're not really involved, they're just having a "relationship."

Anyway, I'm not ready to hook up with anyone right now. The way it is between us is totally cool, so let's not mess it up with ownership. Okay? Let's keep it loose and easy. (*Pause.*) Okay. Cool.

(*Checking her watch.*) Wow. I gotta go. I gotta get this Alpo home because I have a "relationship" with my dog. See ya.

DINAH

Dinah knows from experience that it pays to be cyber safe.

Hey, it all started out this innocent thing. I mean, I'm on the Internet almost every night, so I'm, like, What can it hurt to chat, you know? What can be the danger of chatting with someone thousands of miles away? So I started up this correspondence with this guy named Boris who lived in Bristol, England. We chatted almost every night for three months.

At first, it was all very innocent. We exchanged stuff about our ages and hobbies and favorite movies and music and stuff. But little by little—and I should have known better—it started getting more and more personal. But I figured . . . I mean the guy was five thousand miles away. Anyway, we got into to some pretty personal stuff, physical things and sex and . . . well, after a while, there weren't a whole lot of secrets.

When we exchanged pictures on-line I was, like, wow! Boris was buff, had a six-pack, was really cute. And a teenager, just like me. When I showed his picture to Janet, I thought she was going to die.

But after a while, things started to get out of hand. He started getting pretty raunchy. The night he sent me porno, I

15

knew it was time to sign off. I tried to let him down easy. Told him I was too busy with school work and that, and stopped answering him. After a while, I stopped hearing from him. Whew. I was really glad it was over. But it wasn't.

One evening, coming back from cheerleading practice, this man gets out of his car and blocks my way. When I tried to get past, he grabs me by the arms and starts pulling me toward his car. I screamed. I've never been so frightened. Thank God some of the guys at football practice heard me and came running over from the field. They jumped the guy and pinned him and I called the cops on my cell. It was Boris. And he wasn't a teenager. He was this strange looking man who was about fifty years old. Turned out he was wanted in England for raping more than twenty girls he'd set up on the Internet.

Let me tell you: Don't, whatever you do, chat with strangers or send out any information about yourself over the Net. Take my advice . . . only talk to people you know.

SPENCER

Carly has been talking about Spencer behind her back, a practice that has backfired due to the fact that Spencer has been told by a girl who couldn't keep it secret. To say Spencer is unhappy is greatly understating the case—she's hurt and furious.

No . . . you shut up, okay? You just shut the hell up and listen. There's no excuse. So don't try to cop-out with all your best excuses because I'm not believing you because you're a lying back-stabbing, gossipy bitch. I saw the expression on your face, and I knew right away you were lying. Your face was on fire with embarrassment. *(Pause.)* Shut up, I said. Cool it . . . And you claim to be my best friend. Hey, a best friend doesn't go behind my back spreading rumors about me sleeping around. Where you get this stuff, anyway? And, even if it were true, if you were a real friend, you'd never tell. To go around hanging out stories like this, to . . . Let me ask you, Carly, what you get outta messing with someone's life? Outta causing them pain and trouble? You realize what you've done to my reputation?

And we've been buds since junior high. Tight. Best friends. At least, this is what I thought. And now you go and ruin it by saying bad things behind my back.

You think I don't know what's behind it? You think I'm lame? It all Christian Barry, isn't it? The fact that you were hot for him and now he's dating me. (*Pause*.) Bull . . . .! Hey, look, you had every chance with him and I was totally cool. It was nothing to me. Like it's my fault he calls me and asks me out? At first I turned him down because I didn't want to get in the way, but when he told me he wasn't interested in you . . . I remember now, yeah, I remember how silent you got when I told you he called me. I should have known right then you were pissed. Why didn't you say something instead of planting rumors and making me look bad to the whole school?

You hurt me, Carly. You did a bad thing. Friends don't turn on friends. I hope you're happy. I hope you feel proud. I hope you got thrills outta your rotten lie. Now, get away from me, far away, and stay away. I don't wanna become infected.

SALDANA

Even though she's an accomplished musician, Saldana is not ready for band. Here she relates her reservations about becoming a member:

You know how long I've been playing the clarinet? Since I was ten. Since I was this high (*She indicates.*) They used to sit me on telephone books so I could see the music. And it was easy for me. From the beginning. Why, I don't know. I just took to the instrument.

I've won all kind of prizes and stuff. Next month I'm going to Detroit for a recital. Eventually, after college, I wanna play in a symphony orchestra.

Because I'm good, Mr. Bostford is always after me to join the band. He keeps bugging me and calling my parents and, now, they're bugging me too. But band sucks. I know, because I went to a couple of rehearsals. You can't believe how awful it was. First thing is, most of the kids can't play, they just rent an instrument. Me? I practice three hours a day.

At the first rehearsal it took them four hours to figure out "Stars and Stripes Forever" because most of the kids could barely read music. And nobody played in tune. And their time was awful: The brass would be playing ahead of the beat, the woodwinds behind, the percussion way off in another county. You've heard these bands, you know how they sound. Like a whole bunch of geese turned loose in a can factory.

At the second rehearsal they handed out uniforms. I'm a two and they gave me a tent. The pants were so long it looked like my legs were melting. The sleeves were so long, for a minute I thought I'd lost my hands. Scary. It's bad enough to play with people who're tone-deaf, let alone look like you're part of a clown act.

I've tried to explain this to my parents, but they think I should support the school. But I'm not about to become a dork for anybody. Besides, I just couldn't play that bad if I tried. Unless I traded in my fingers for thumbs.

EVY

Evy tells her sister she's aware of her practice of conning their grandmother.

Let me vent a little here, okay? You think I don't know why you suck up to Grandma like you do? Call her all the time and butter her up like fresh toast? Because you know she's a soft touch, that's why. Because you know she can't say, "No." And, to be real blunt about it, it makes me sick. (*Pause.*) Oh, no, don't deny it, because it's plain for anyone to see. It's so damned obvious. The only person who doesn't see through it is Grandma because she loves you so much. And this is the sick part of it. How you can take advantage of someone like this, your own grandmother, is way beyond me.

Like going to visit her every year right before school starts. You think this isn't transparent? You think that I, everybody else in the family doesn't see through your little scam? You go visit her because you know damn well she's going to feel bad for you and take you out and buy you back-to-school clothes and stuff. Like this last trip . . . you came home with over six-hundred bucks worth of stuff. (*Pause.*) No, no . . . I'm not jealous. Don't try to pull that crap. Don't try to lay that on me. All I am is pissed because you're using her to get favors.

You know what you are, Darla? You're a major, conniving weasel. (*Pause.*) Oh, yeah? Well . . . I'll talk to you any way I want. It's about time somebody does. It's about time somebody around here straightens you out. It's about time you should know that the whole family thinks you're an underhanded brat for taking advantage of an old woman who loves you too much to see the truth.

Look . . . when somebody loves you as much as Grandma does, you don't take advantage. Don't you understand the greatest thing that she gives you isn't new clothes . . . it's her unconditional love? And when you take advantage of this, use it, it's worse than outright stealing. So . . . stop it!

NANCY

A Hollywood producer has expressed interest in a story Nancy wrote. Here she describes her meeting with the man:

A school bud of mine gave this story I wrote to her dad who works in the movie business. He read it and passed it along to this producer—Harry Spears. Guess what? The guy called me and asked me to come to his office. I could've died. My mom wanted to go along, but I thought this would be juvenile, so I went alone.

His office was on the top floor of this high-rise. The view was awesome. The furniture was totally modern—futuristic. It looked fantastic, but you couldn't sit on it. His secretary told me to wait and gave me a glass of Evian with a lemon wedge in it. It was really cool. I felt totally Hollywood. Finally, after about twenty minutes, she takes me into Mr. Spears' office.

When he got up from behind his desk I couldn't believe it—he was just as tall sitting down as he was standing up. He was even shorter than my brother Harold who's a runt. He shook my hand and told me to sit down and was real nice. He kept calling me, "Kid."

He said he thought my story was good and very original and asked me how I felt about working with a professional screenwriter and sharing credits. I told him, "Okay, this would be cool." Then he tells me about some changes they'd like to make. Like instead of having the main character be a cheerleader, have her be this crackhead who gets gang-raped by the basketball team. I told him this wasn't exactly what I had in mind.

When I told him I thought way too many movies showed the bad side of kids and were too violent, I could tell he didn't like it. He said they made movies for the market, that this is what kids today were into.

I told him I wasn't sure, that I'd have to think it over. And I have . . . I'd be embarrassed to be part of junk like that. I think I'll always be.

TAMMY

Tammy is a lucky survivor of an alcohol-related accident.

I . . . I don't know what happened. It just . . . We were driving along and . . . alluva sudden . . . I told him not to drink so much at the party. I warned him. But you couldn't talk to Larry. He had this thing about how much he could drink, how many beers he could pound. It was, like . . . almost like this competitive thing. He had this reputation, you know. About how much he could hold. And he felt he had to live up to it. And the other guys, his buds . . . he was, like, this hero to them and they would egg him on.

I shouldn't have gone with him in the first place. My mom warned me, told me not to. I lied to her. Told her I was going with Janet and Zack.

We got to the party around eight and left a little after midnight. Larry was drunk and crazy and I should have stayed over. But, like fool, I got in the car. I mean . . . I'd ridden with him before, right? As soon as he got behind the wheel he started screaming and singing and showing off and speeding. I told him to slow down, but he wouldn't listen. He just kept going faster. Maybe eight or ninety. Really fast.

We ran the stop sign at Pleasant Street and the stop light at Elm and almost hit a car. We ran up over the curb a couple of times. I was scared to death. I knew we were in serious trouble. I kept screaming at him to slow down and stop, but he wouldn't pay any attention. He was totally wired. I tried to grab the keys, but I couldn't get them out of the ignition.

The last thing I remember was us jumping the curb and going off into this field and branches and trees and stuff flying past the car. The noise was like thunder. That's the last thing I remember till I woke up in the ambulance.

Larry lived a few days on life support. He never gained consciousness. The whole thing was a nightmare. Still is. I don't know if I'll ever get over it.

JASMINE

Jasmine has taken a summer job with a major department store. At first she was thrilled, but now, after a few days on the job, she's disenchanted, discovering the meaning of the word "work." Here she complains to the personnel person who hired her:

Yeah, but you didn't tell me all this other stuff went along with the job. I was supposed to be a sales associate, remember? (*Pause.*) No you didn't. You didn't say that. No way. (*Pause.*) Well, if you did, I didn't hear it. All I heard was that I was to start in the cosmetics department. (*Pause.*) But it's been three weeks and I'm still in the stock room. You know what I did all day yesterday? All day? I put security tags on five hundred pair of jeans. What's this have to do with cosmetics? And the day before I got stuck folding towels for the linen department. I even missed my lunch hour because someone phoned in sick. Sick, hell. She probably got tipped off on the towel folding job. Oh, yeah, and that's another thing. Where do you find these people? The girl I worked next to yesterday had BO so bad I could puke. The smell's just gotta be in the towels for life.

You're gonna have to run a BO closeout to get rid of 'em. And I always thought this was a high-class operation.

Check out at my hands. (*Displaying her hands.*) This is from putting on those damned security tags. Just look. I could be a mine worker. This isn't what I expected, Vanessa. (*Pause.*) I don't care about learning retail from the ground up, all I wanna do is sell cosmetics. Besides, what I've been doing since I started work here is *below* ground. All I am is a glorified stock boy. What next, am I gonna have to unload a semi full of bricks? I think maybe I'm outta here.(*Pause.*) Huh? I get how much discount on clothes? (*Pause.*) That much? I thought you said twenty-five percent. I guess I didn't hear that either. (*Pause.*) Forty percent off? Wow.

Know what, Vanessa? . . . I think maybe I'll hang in for a while.

TRINA

No longer able to live with her father's rejection, Trina has traveled a great distance to confront him and gain understanding.

Look, Dad, I've come a thousand miles. And I'm not leaving till we talk. If I have to sleep here on your doorstep, this is where I'll be till you open up and let me in. I'm *not* leaving, dammit! (*Pause.*) Okay. (*She steps into the house, noting the surroundings.*) Not bad. A little different from Indiana. Since when are you into modern? (*Pause.*) Oh, Bunny likes it. Bunny? Jesus Dad, for God's sake. Bunny? You left us for someone named Bunny? I won't tell Mom. She'd really freak. (*Pause.*) How'd I get here? I hitched it. Was picked up by some pretty strange dudes. This one perv guy, outside Tulsa, tried to put the moves on me. He was one of the Big Hands People, you know. Well . . . he won't be able to uncross his legs for a while.

(*Stalks around, observing.*) My own, square father living with Frank Lloyd Wright. Amazing. Guess this is what they mean by the mid-life blowout. (*Pause.*) Okay, so I'm sarcastic. So what? What the hell you expect for Christ's sake? That I'm supposed to love the fact that you walked out without a word and moved to California with someone you met at a daycare center? What the hell you expect? (*Pause.*) I don't wanna hear that. That's bull. So you were unhappy. Who isn't? Like you got the market cornered on unhappiness? You got any idea how much hurt you caused? (*Pause.*) No, you don't. You can't put yourself in someone else's shoes. You got no idea how it affected me, Mom, David—all of us. And leaving cold like that. And the fact that you cut us off completely, not returning my phone calls, my emails, or letters. Do you hate me this much? Am I this worthless? (*Pause.*) Oh, yeah . . .why wouldn't I think so? And don't tell me you love me. You don't treat someone you love like bad breath? The leaving's one thing, the rejection's another. Knowing your own father doesn't give a damn if you live or die, this is the worst part. How could you do it? How could you do it to me, Dad? Tell me. Answer me. How the hell could you could do it?

STEPHIE

Stephie, outside her mother's hospital room, tells of her emphysema and of losing the battle with cancer.

I have to talk softly because I'm here in the hallway outside my mom's room. They made me get out while they examine her. She's in here for emphysema. She has it bad. It's because she's been a smoker since she was a teenager. Now she can hardly breathe. She has to gasp for every breath and has to have this oxygen with her every place she goes. The last time she was here they took out part of her lung.

From the time I was little I remember her with a cigarette in her hand; while she was driving, doing housework, reading—it was her constant companion. Her death sentence, I should say. My dad tried to get her to stop smoking lots of times, and sometimes, for a while, she would. But then she'd start up again. Our house still smells like smoke. I think the stuff works its way into the foundation.

We first thought something was wrong when Mom developed this hacking cough that got worse and worse. It got to the point where she'd go into a coughing spasm for minutes. We all knew it was from cigarettes. Finally, Dad insisted that she go in for a checkup. They found cancer. They operated right away and removed almost all of one lung. She's never been the same. She's been going downhill steadily ever since.

She used to be beautiful and active and alive. Now she's wasted away to nothing. You wouldn't believe it if you saw her. She's almost a skeleton. It breaks my heart. She hasn't got long to live, we all know that. She knows too, but she never complains. She keeps smiling through it all.

I used to smoke, too, till this happened. I thought I was cool. Thank God I woke up to the fact that I'd be *really* cool when they put me in the ground.

MIKI

During her initial visit with a psychologist, Miki speaks of her rape, her the lingering fears, anxieties, and depression.

I've tried to get over it. You think I haven't tried? But I can't. Not yet, anyway. Maybe . . . maybe in time. I don't know. It's like . . . like . . . I haven't slept in my room since he raped me. I'm still sleeping on a cot in my mom and dad's room. And they're cool with it. They understand. Thank God for them. My family, my friends have been fantastic. And I know sometimes it isn't easy for them, I know I've been out of it a lot and sassy and bitchy. I'm still in shock, depressed and shaking inside. I should be over it, I guess. Maybe. I don't know. Maybe you never get over it. I know one thing for sure—my life has been changed forever.

I knew better than to sleep with the sliding door all the way open. I usually open it just a crack and put this door lock on it, you know. But I figured . . . I mean . . . nothing like this could happen in our neighborhood. Boy, was I ever wrong. I know now that no neighborhood is out of danger.

I didn't hear him come in. I'm a very sound sleeper. But then I sensed something, you know. Something made me feel uneasy. When I looked up, there he was, standing over me like this giant shadow. Before I could react or scream he was on me with his hand over my mouth and a knife at my neck. He said if I made a sound he'd slit my throat. Then he took this hunk of duct tape out of his pocket and taped my mouth shut. I didn't move. I was sure he was going to kill me or drag me out of the house. He was heavy on me and I closed my eyes and tried to think of something else, anything to get my mind off what was happening to me.

When he left, I just lay there shaking. And I'm still shaking inside. Like I said . . . my life's been changed forever.

THELMA

Thelma's temporary crush was perfect except for one unsavory personal problem—halitosis. Here Thelma discusses the problem with friend Elaine:

I met this dreamy guy at Macy's. At the cosmetics counter. Blond. Built. Really sexy. He looked like a soap actor. (*As an aside.*) I understand a lot of those guys are gay. Anyway . . . this guy, Carson—even his name was cool—he says, "Nice shoes." I was wearing the thongs. Right away this was impressive. Most guys never check your styles, just your butt and boobs. So, this was impressive right there. We started talking about school and stuff and the fact I'd never seen him around. Turns out he'd just moved here from Boston. One thing leads to another and he asks me out. (*Pause.*) I know, I know I shoulda known more about him, but . . . Anyway, he picks me up in one of those old Porsches. You know, the kind that looks like a bathtub?

I get in the car and this is the first time I notice it—this real bad odor. It was like a mixture and rotten meat and month-old milk. I thought maybe it was something to do with the car, a muffler, or something. Whatever. At first, I didn't connect it to him. You kidding? The way he looked? But when we're at the movie, I knew it was him. His breath was unreal. I guess I hadn't noticed it at Macy's because of all the cosmetics. I did my best to avoid him, holding my hand up to my face, turning away, scrunching down in my seat.

At dinner it was cool because he was sitting across the table from me. I kept staring at him. I couldn't believe someone this good looking could have breath that'd shatter glass. Now comes the worst part: When we pull up in front of my place, he leans over to kiss me. Kiss me, Elaine. (*Cringes.*) Ugh. Here I got this human garbage can heading for me. It was bizarre. I freaked. (*Pause.*) What'd I do? I went into this coughing fit and jumped out of the car. I told him I'd just gotten over the flu, walking pneumonia, was still probably carrying germs. I kept coughing all the way into my house.

I haven't seen Carson since. Hey, I wouldn't have to see him anyway . . . I could smell him coming.

ASHLEY

Ashley argues in favor of abstinence with a resistant friend.

. . . okay, but I don't agree. You're whole argument is totally bogus. To be real straight about it, the whole "using protection" thing makes me wanna vomit. It's, like, total crap. Like the stuff they put out at school (*Quoting mockingly, sing-song, with derision.*): "If you're sexually active, always use a latex condom, not a natural skin one. Stay away from oil-based lubricants—they weaken condoms—and stick with the water-based ones." Can you believe this? How about sticking with nothing and saying, "No"? "No" is the only foolproof contraceptive on earth. (*Pause.*) The hell you can't. (*Pause.*) So it's a natural urge, so what? So you back off. So you go so far and cool it. (*Pause.*) Our parents? Sure, of course kids had sex back then, but it wasn't out of hand, it wasn't making it with every person you meet. Besides, in those days people looked down on it, it wasn't a given that it was okay to go sleeping around. Today . . . forget it. It's no wonder there are over three million cases of sexually transmitted diseases among teens today. Hell, Lacy . . . seems like nobody can say "No" anymore. (*Pause.*) Well . . . you can follow you "natural urges" all you want. It's your life. But how 'bout the consequences? AIDS. Gonorrhea. Getting pregnant. Is it worth it?

Look . . . God knows I'm not perfect. I mean . . . hey, I get urges too. And sometime it's not easy. I mean, I get pressure like everybody else, you know. And it's hard. You wanna give in. But I'm not going to because the odds are too great. I wanna screw up my life at this age? I don't think so. (*Pause.*) Well, hey, whatever's right, okay? It's your body. But don't come crying to me when you're buying maternity clothes.

ANNEMARIE

Annemarie tells her long-time friend, Jackie, that their relationship is over.

(*Catching up with Jackie.*) Hey, Jackie, wait up a minute. (*Pause.*) Jackie, I know you're in a hurry, but I have to talk to you, okay? Look . . . it's hard from me to tell you this, but I just have to. And I thought it'd be best if I told you to your face. Jackie, you've been a good friend, but I just don't feel the same about our friendship anymore. (*Pause.*) Just hold on. Let me finish. Lots of stuff has happened lately that really upsets me, a lot of . . . (*Pause.*) If you'll stop interrupting, I'll tell you. Okay? Okay? Jeez.

First off, you've turned against me. (*Pause.*) Yes you have. For some reason you've turned against me. You and Carol and Danielle. It's like I'm not part of you guys anymore. I knew something was going on the other day when I sat down with you guys at lunch. When I talked, tried to get in on the conversation, you all acted like I wasn't there, totally ignored me. How you think this made me feel? This really hurt. And the next day you all ignored me again. It's like alluva sudden you dumped me completely. I can understand it with Carol and

39

Danielle, but you, Jackie? Hey, we've been friends since grade school. (*Pause.*) Please, let me finish.

I know what's behind it. I'm one of the "not-so-popular" kids. You think I don't know this? I know I'm quiet and not outgoing and don't have a lot of clothes. I know all this. But I've been like this since we were little kids. I guess now, though, in high school, I'm an embarrassment, right? Well . . . I can't change the basic me, Jackie. I can't help being shy.

Anyway, I just wanted to tell you straight out how I feel. And as far as the way I dress is concerned, it's the best I can do because it's all I can afford. Besides, I think what's inside the package is a lot more important than the wrapper.

Goodbye, Jackie.

TRISHA

Trisha speaks with a nurse outside the room of her recently deceased brother:

When Mom and Dad told me he had AIDS, I couldn't believe it. It was the biggest shock I've ever had. I mean, these things happen to other people, other families.

Up till this time, I just thought life was all about clothes and music and friends and partying. I never thought about it seriously, not really. But when you get hit with something like this, when it's personal, you look at things differently. You realize that life isn't all new styles and cars and boyfriends. Life takes on this whole different meaning. Especially when you know someone you love only has a few months to live.

Charlie and I were never really that close. He was a lot older. He moved to Chicago when I was still in junior high and only came home during the holidays. I never thought about him much one way or the other. Until I realized I was never going to see him again. Then the word "brother" took on this whole new meaning. I mean . . . he was part of me. My *brother!*

When it got to the point he couldn't take care of himself, Charlie moved back home. He was super-skinny and very weak. We looked after him. Near the end he insisted we bring him here. He didn't want to be a bother. Here he was dying and thinking about other people. Is this neat, or what? And he was, like, the only one who wasn't sad and depressed.

I'd never seen anyone die before. It was real peaceful. Mom and Dad are sill in there.

Even though this whole thing has been pretty awful, I think it's helped me because, for the first time in my life, I've learned about caring, about putting somebody else first. And, you know, now I don't feel like a teenager anymore, I feel more like a woman.

MARY

She enters with three, helium-filled balloons that she uses to as props to dramatize a monologue dealing with letting go of emotional baggage.

After my mom and dad split up, I had all kinds of hang-ups. I'd sit in my room all day with the drapes drawn. My mom did everything she could to help me, but nothing worked, and I just kept getting more and more depressed every day.

The thing was, I blamed myself for my mom and dad breaking up. I knew a lot of their problem was me, because I was into crack and drinking and hanging with a bad crowd. They had these terrible fights over it. My dad said my mom set a bad example, and my mom said it was his fault for traveling all the time and not being a better father. It was awful.

Then, one day, while I was in the park, this old woman came over and sat down beside me. She was real friendly. We talked and—I don't know why—I told her everything. She said she'd felt the same way after her husband died—blamed herself for not being a better wife. Then she told me how she got over it. She said she made up her mind not to be guilty and sad and depressed because all that didn't change anything. She said she had to learn to let go of all the guilt and blame and negative stuff that was pulling her down. She said it was, like, a thing of mind over matter. She said I had to let go.

There was this guy in the park selling balloons. The lady went over and bought three and said, "You gotta let go of the bad stuff, let it float up out of sight and out of your life." She was amazing. She handed me the balloons. She said, "Okay, now, the first thing we're going to let go of is guilt. So, say, 'Good-bye, guilt' and let go of a balloon and watch the guilt fly away."

So I did. I said, "Good-bye guilt," and let go of one of the balloons (*She releases a balloon and it rises and floats away.*)

"Now," she said, "let go of all your negative thoughts."
I said, "Good-bye, negative stuff," and let go of another balloon. (*She releases another balloon and watches it rise.*)

"Now, anger," she said.

"I said, "Good-bye anger," and let go of the last balloon and watched the anger fly away. (*She releases the final balloon.*)

And it worked. It was awesome. I made up my mind to let go of all of the bad stuff and watch it fly outta my life. The only thing I blame myself for now, is not letting go a whole lot sooner.

LEE ANN

Lee Anne describes the rigors of her driver's test to friend, Doris.

It's a wonder I passed. I was totally freaked during the whole thing. From the time of the exam till I got through with the driving part. I'd gone over the booklet twenty times, had it aced, you know. But when I got down there, I was a total blank. And I didn't wanna take a chance on cheating. Although this guy next to me had his whole family helping him with the questions. I coulda sworn I failed, but I only missed two—the speed limit in alleyways and the distance you have to stay behind emergency vehicles. Stupid questions, anyhow. Who's gonna speed down an alleyway? (*Pause.*) Big deal. So you got a hundred, so what? You drive like a spaz. (*Pause.*) You do, too. If you're so good, how come you never parallel park? (*Pause.*) No way. Last time we went for pizza you parked in the Wal-Mart lot and there was a space right in front of the place. You can't park, Doris. It's one thing to ace the test, it's another to know how to drive. Anyway . . . it was a totally scary thing.

Of course I had to go with my dad, right? He had to be in on it. This made it even worse. All the way down there he's, like, laying all these scary statistics on me: Crashes are the leading cause of death among teenagers; fatal crashes are more likely to happen when other teenagers are in the car; speed is usually the reason teens have fatal crashes; the nighttime fatal crash rate for teens is twice as high than during the day. Then he went into his usual thing about the high cost of insurance because I'd be driving. It's, like, my driving is gonna put the family in the poor house, you know. By the time we get there—I'm a zombie.

The guy who gave me the driving part had the personality of an oyster. He was all serious. A totally weird nerd: Hush Puppy shoes, clip-on tie—you know the type. He sat there with his clipboard and never smiled. "Turn right. Turn left. Park here. Back up. Slow down." He was a two-word person. When he gets home at night, I'll bet the only thing he says to his wife all evening is, "Let's eat."

I don't know how I passed, but I did. I finally got my license. All I have to do now is figure out how to pay for the extra insurance.

MAUREEN

Maureen is fed up with her mother's profligate behavior, her abandoning her household, her motherly duties—behavior that has resulted in Maureen assuming the mantle of homemaker and caretaker.

I'm tired, fed up, I've had it with being a house slave and babysitter while you're out jacking around with your boy-friend-of-the-week. (*Pause.*) So, I'm a smart mouth, so what? You deserve it for being a part-time, jerk-off mother! (*Pause.*) Hey, you don't scare me. Remember, I'm bigger than you and, besides—I'm not hung over. You come stumbling in here drunk at two o'clock in the morning, bouncing off the walls, dropping stuff . . . This is sickening, "mother dearest." And it's way past wearing thin—it's *threadbare.* I could turn you in big time, you know that, don't you? (*Pause.*) No, I'm not going to, but I could. I'm going to save you the embarrassment and let you keep your self-esteem—if you've got any left, that is. (*Pause.*)

Yeah. You got it right—I'm pissed. Good and pissed. I come home from school to a house that looks like it's been A-bombed: clothes all over the place, dishes in the sink, beds unmade. And I'm supposed to . . . hey, what the hell you think I am, room service? You're a drunken, uncaring, negligent mother who leans on her teenage daughter because you can't face up to life. It's no wonder Dad left. I don't know how he put up with your crap as long as he did.

Are you listening me? (*Pause.*) Okay. Good. Starting right now, this minute, you return to being a full-time mother instead of a full-time jerk, because I'm giving notice—I quit! I'm returning to my role as a teenager with a life and friends and homework I can turn in on time because I'm no longer going to be a scrubwoman and a full time babysitter to a little brother who hasn't had any motherly love or attention in over a year.

If you wanna carry this further, I'll be in my room doing my algebra. In the meantime, there's a number on the fridge. I wrote it down for you. You're going to call it. Today! It's AA.

MELODY

Melody warns her friend of the addictive dangers of drug use.

It's your life, Sally. If you wanna mess it up bad, go ahead. You start using, you're gonna get into it and you won't be able to get off. I know, I went through it. I know how drugs hook you and, then, how you'll do anything to get 'em. You start out like I did, thinking it's cool. This is the way it was when Bobby got me into using. I was just going along, you know. I mean, I wanted to have friends and be accepted. I didn't care who I was with, I just needed to be around a lot of people. I figured the quickest way was to use. Anyway, I didn't give a damn. After my dad died, my stepmother became this abusive bitch. I was lost, just like you.

Bobby's parents were losers, and he was real down and I could relate to him. Anyway, I was ready. I was an easy sell. Besides, what harm could it do, you know. This is the way it starts out, like this innocent thing. Bobby first got me into Ecstasy. Ecstasy made me feel like I didn't have a problem in the world. What Bobby didn't tell me is is that I would want to take it all the time and that I'd feel like I couldn't live without it. After a while . . . I couldn't. I started to steal and cut classes to get high. Yeah, feeling good meant that I had to cheat, lie, and steal.

When I was high, I felt like everything was cool. You get this false feeling that everything's okay. But it wasn't. I was twitching and having terrible headaches and eye spasms and I was grinding my teeth like crazy. The side effects were bizarre. My health nurse saw the signs and helped me get into recovery. I'm still in detox.

So, do yourself a humongous favor—don't let anyone talk you into drugs in any way shape or form. Oh, yeah, by the way . . . Bobby OD'd last Friday.

RUTH

Ruth finds a day on the trail exhausting, disgusting and a complete waste of her time.

(*Panting.*) Hey, Sal . . . I gotta rest (*Pause.*) How come? How come? How come, is that if I walk another foot I'm going to swallow my heart. We've been walking now for over two hours. Up hill. Over ruts and rocks. Through mud. Through bushes and thickets and brambles. Look at my legs. Totally scratched and bleeding. If I'd known this, I would've stayed at the lodge and watched TV. (*Pause.*) No you didn't. No way. You told me it was a nice little hike to Lake Pyramid. Everybody does it, you said. Yeah, everybody who's made it to the top of Mt. Everest. Are you nuts?

(*She removes a boot and sock. She wiggles her toes while observing her foot.*) Holy crap! My foot looks like pot roast. (*Pause.*) The hell it doesn't. It's these stupid, damn boots I rented. (*Pause.*) Tenderfoot? (*Waving her boot at him.*) How about shutting your face before I give you a tender head? I should have known better. I'm just not cut out for outdoors stuff. Walking around in ten-pound boots, eating cold beans, sleeping in your clothes. It isn't my thing.

I'm heading back. (*Pause.*) The hell I'm not. I'm outta here. (*Pause.*) I don't care if it's harder going down than up. At least I'll be heading for civilization, for burgers and fries instead of trail-mix and squeezing water out of a leaf. (*She puts on her sock and boot.*)

The more I think about it—exercise sucks. What's it get you? Aches and pains and broken bones. It's a total waste when you can be at the mall sucking up shakes and making fun of people. Like look at you. You've always got something hurting. And you're supposed to be in such great shape. You know what I think, Sal? I think you're in such great shape you're going to be dead by the time you're twenty.

I'll be waiting in the SUV. (*She exits.*)

BONNIE

When Carma confronts Bonnie regarding her weight problem, Bonnie responds honestly out of deep concern for her best friend.

Okay, Carma, you asked me, so I'll tell you. Yes—you're too heavy. C'mon, do I have to tell you? You know you're way overweight. Why you think you asked me the question in the first place? If I'm being honest here, do you think I'm going to say you're a size two? You *have* a weight problem, *have* had a weight problem and will *continue* to have a weight problem unless you drop M&M's as a staple food. It's crazy.

Look, so long as we're into it, I may as well be totally upfront. You're too heavy and it's affecting your life. How come you're the class comic? Why you think? Because this is how you cover up for how you really feel about yourself. Down deep inside, I mean, for being so heavy. Nobody your age with your weight problem can be truly happy, Carm.

You gotta learn to push away the food and stop eating junk. I've seen how you eat. This isn't normal. It's, like, you're starving, or something. And then you finish up what's on other people's plates. This is disgusting, Car. Sorry, but it really is.

And you can't go on laughing it off and making excuses and pretending it doesn't matter. It does. And it affects how other people relate to you. Boys in particular.

You can call yourself plus-size, full-bodied, heavy, large, full-figured, whatever, but it still boils down to one thing—fat. You know it, and I know it. And other kids know it too.

Hey, everybody likes you, Carm. You're really neat and fun to be around and no matter what, skinny or heavy, I'll always be your friend. This won't change. But *you* have to change. Why be overweight when you don't have to be? It's all a matter of getting a better self-image and saying no to Twinkies. And if you're unhappy, tell me about it, get it out, okay?

Look, Carm, I love you. I just want you to start loving yourself.

ROXY

Roxy, adversely affected by a bad home life, spills her feelings to her high-school counselor.

(*Wiping here eyes with a Kleenex.*) I'm sorry . . . I . . . It's just that, that . . . I don't know *what* to do. (*Pause.*) It's okay. I'll be all right. Give me a second. (*Blows her nose, wipes away tears.*) There. (*Pause.*) It's just *so* awful. I can't tell you. I don't know what to do.

My parents—they separated a couple of years ago—fought all the time. Mostly because of my mother. She was smoking a lot of dope and would lie about it. My dad would find it hidden around the house. Finally he moved out and they got a divorce. Then last year, my mom married this guy named Rick. He's a lot younger and has a crack habit and shoplifts then returns things to get money for his habit. I hate him. He sits around the house all day watching TV and smoking. He's a total slob. And he barely speaks to me. When he does, every other word is the F word. He scares me a lot. I don't trust him. When my brother—he's two years older than me—threatened to kill him, Mom made him move. Now I'm home alone with Rick a lot. I stay in my room with the door locked.

Yesterday, I found out Rick and my mom were doing drugs together. I found this stuff in their nightstand. I know I shouldn't be nosing around, but, the way it is, can anyone blame me? When I told Mom, she went crazy and started screaming and calling me a bitch and worse and Rick said he was going to "beat my little ass." He came after me and I ran out of the house. I'm afraid to go back and get my stuff. I can't. I won't. And my dad's in Mexico on business. I don't know what to do. I just don't know . . . (*She breaks into sobs. Pause. She recovers somewhat.*) I'm sorry . . . (*Pause.*) You will? I can stay with you till my dad gets back? Really? You mean it? (*Pause.*) Oh, God, thank you, Ms. Wright. Thank you.

ABBY

Abby tells Karen about the experience of shopping for used cars with her father.

Boy, are you lucky. Your dad was cool. You didn't have to go through it. You got a new Honda. But I was driving my brother's burned-out Camaro. A classic. A classic piece of junk. This black cloud came out of the tailpipe, and when I turned off the engine, it backfired. It was totally embarrassing. No wonder I was bummed.

Of course my dad has to shop for the best deal. And forget about new. When I mentioned a new Mustang he goes, "Why buy a new car when you can pick up a used car that's just as good for a lot less money?" Yeah, right. Used is always better than new. Sure. If this is the case, why didn't he buy a used Ford instead of a new Lexus?

So we run around to all these used car lots looking for a deal. We must have gone to every lot on Automobile Row. Pretty much all the same—a bunch of balloons and pennants with an army of weasels for salesmen. You pull in and they fall on you like from parachutes.

This first guy was an over-friendly dork with a bad comb-over that made him look like Hitler. According to him, every car on the lot was perfect, low-mileage, only driven to church on Sundays by Mother Teresa. He had this odd twitch, and when he smiled, you could see what he had for lunch. Totally discussing.

It was like this every place we went. And, of course, my dad had to haggle. Haggle, haggle, haggle. I got the feeling he would haggle if they gave the car away. Mom says haggling is a man thing. So he haggled with weasels and kicked tires and looked under hoods for five hours. He almost bought an Explorer, but backed out when the guy wouldn't throw in new floor mats. They cost thirty dollars. Like Mom says—it's a man thing.

When we got home, Mom yelled at him good and told him to grow up and stop being a macho idiot. She really let him have it good.

I pick up my new Mustang on Thursday.